the ikigai book

Finding happiness and Purpose the Japanese way

Linda Davidsson

contents

introduction

Congratulations on purchasing *The Ikigai Book,* and thank you for doing so.

The following chapters will discuss the concept of ikigai. This Japanese concept is all about helping people figure out what their purpose is in life to help them live happier lives.

For starters, we'll see exactly what ikigai is all about. Then we'll dive into the Japanese philosophy behind the concept of ikigai, including the four pillars on which it stands.

We'll cover the idea of *the reason for getting up* (something you'll hear mentioned a lot when talking about ikigai), and it's this that'll become your ikigai. Your reason for getting up is what motivates you to continue working towards your ultimate goal.

After that, we'll examine how to figure out what *your* ikigai is. There are many different ways to discover this. Everybody will have their own way of discovering their ikigai, so the most important thing is to take the time for the self-reflection you need to discover yours.

Next, we'll look at the importance of happiness. Ikigai is all about being happy with your life, so happiness plays a big role in all of this. If your ikigai doesn't spark happiness, then there is a good chance that it's not really your ikigai.

Then we'll talk about meditation. Japanese people are big

proponents of meditation, and meditation can go a long way in helping you discover what your ikigai is.

Lastly, we'll go over acceptance and accepting yourself. Ikigai teaches us that self-acceptance is the key to life and happiness.

There are plenty of books on this subject on the market; thanks again for choosing this one! Every effort was made to ensure it's full of as much useful information as possible. Please enjoy!

one
the history of ikigai

LET'S get this out of the way: Ikigai is pronounced "ee-key-guy." Ikigai is a concept created by the Japanese that brings two of their concepts together. The first is "iki," meaning *life* or *alive*, and the second is "gai," meaning *worth* and *benefit*. When those two things are brought together, it means "that which gives your life worth, meaning, or purpose." It's very similar to what the French call "raison d'etre" or "reason for being."

There's some evidence that suggests the word dates back to the Heian period. The clinical psychologist Akihiro Hasegawa wrote a paper in 2001 explaining that "gai" came from the word "kai," which means "shell." During the Heian period, shells were thought to be of extreme value. You can also see this in other Japanese works, like hatarakigai, which means "the value of work." They also have yarigai-ga Aru, which translates to "it's worth doing."

The concept is thought to have started within the basic wellness and health beliefs of Japanese medicine practices. Through medical traditions, they taught that physical wellbeing is connected with our sense of purpose and mental-emotional health.

The word ikigai was also referenced in the Gordon Mathews book "*What Makes Life Worth Living? How Japanese and Amer-*

icans Make Sense of Their Worlds." He explained that the first time that he found the word was back in the 1980s while he lived in Japan, and he believed that:

"The term has a long history, appearing as far back as the 14th century Taiheiki, as well as in such early 20th century works as Natsume Soeki's 1912 novel Kojin; but the contemporary Japanese works on ikigai that I've studied say little about the history of the term or about ikigai as conceived in the past."

The Japanese psychologist Michiki Kumano has explained that ikigai has to do with a state of well-being that is found through devoting oneself to things that you enjoy doing, which helps to make a person feel fulfilled. People have further distinguished this from the idea of transitory pleasure and show its connections to eudaimonia. Eudaimonia is the Greek word that helps explain the sense of life well-lived, which can create a state of happiness that lasts forever.

People have also found a connection between ikigai and CBT, or "Cognitive Behavioral Therapy," because there is an emphasis on doing things that helps a person have a sense of mastery and enjoyment. This is a direct connection with finding ways to help improve feelings of depression. Ken Mogi, a neuroscientist, explained that ikigai is an important and common concept in Japan, which could be translated to "a reason to get up in the morning." It has also been said in a more poetic way with "waking up to joy."

There's also a connection between ikigai and the idea of flow that Mihaly Csikszentmihalyi, a psychologist, created. Mihaly said that flow was something that occurred when a person got in the "zone," such as the state that high-performing athletes perform in. Flow is simply when you are in the moment, and you are fully working your best on things that you like. These moments are more likely to occur "when a person's body or mind is stretched to its limit, in a voluntary effort to accomplish something difficult and worthwhile."

You could say that flow happens when you work on something that you like and you're good at, with the added benefit of adding value to your life and the lives of others. When you look at it this way, you could see flow as being what your ikigai is or an activity that gives your life meaning.

You should also understand that ikigai isn't typically talked about as the purpose a person has in life, but in regards to others and society as well. While there has been a shift in its meaning, ikigai is often viewed as a personal pursuit along with a pursuit to help others. Simply put, ikigai is all about bringing fulfillment, meaning, and purpose to your life while helping the lives of others.

Furthermore, everybody has their own ikigai. Their ikigai is the intersection of talent, the potential to help, and passion. All you have to do is discover what your ikigai is. The journey you take to discover your ikigai will take some time, effort, and self-reflection, but it's something that everybody should and can do.

Now, let's consider the etymology of the word. Gai has to do with finding your value or purpose in life. One of the best ways to understand the ideology of ikigai is to learn about the Venn diagram that represents ikigai.

The idea is that ikigai represents both social and personal ideas. In the ikigai Venn diagram, there are overlapping spheres that represent:

- "What you love."
- "What you are good at."
- "What the world needs."
- "What you can get paid for."

In the middle, where all of these overlap, is what your ikigai is. Ikigai is at the center of everything. It's made up of all of the biggest and most important parts of your life and how they all overlap and work together. When you are working towards learning what your ikigai is, you'll have to work through every one of those areas with honest answers based on your world understanding, your experiences, and your self-knowledge.

When you are working through these sections, some of the information will be easy for you to figure out. Then there'll be sections that'll take some more time and self-reflection. No matter what, filling out an ikigai Venn diagram can help you to figure out where you stand in life and to figure out what your ikigai is. Let's work through the diagram.

- You Love It

In this section, you'll add the things in your life that include what you do or the experiences you have that fill you with a sense of joy. The things that you love could include reading books, hanging out with friends, swimming, writing poetry, hiking, singing, and more.

The most important thing to keep in mind is that you think deeply about everything that you love, without worrying about what your skill level is, if the world needs it, or if it can make you money.

- You Do It Well

In this section, you'll place all of the things that you do fairly well, like your talents, skills that you have developed, hobbies, and more. Things you are good at could range from playing an instrument to performing brain surgery.

Again, when you are filling out this section, don't think about whether you're in love with doing that, if the world needs it, or if it can make you money. Simply list out the things you can do well.

- It Could Help the World

The world can be a big world, but it doesn't have to be. It

could refer to all of humanity, or it could be a small community or anything in between. What the world needs will be decided upon by your impression of the world or what you know others have said they need. The needs of the world might be the need for clean drinking water, heating, nursing, homes, and more.

In this section, you'll have to think explicitly with others in mind and how you can help them. This should go way beyond what your needs are and into how others can be helped.

- Something That Could Make You Money

In this last section, you'll still be thinking about the world, but in a sense that people would be willing to pay you money for it. A person can write amazing poetry or even be great at rock climbing, but those things don't always make them money.

Whether or not you could make money for something you do will depend on several things, such as the economy and the demand for the skill.

Ikigai's Importance

There are several sociologists, journalists, and scientists who have hypothesized and researched how useful and truthful the concept of ikigai is, and they have all come to their own conclusion. There's a theory that ikigai can help you live a longer life.

The Japanese show, "Takeshi no Katai no igaku," partnered with scientists to study the people of Kyotango, which is a town that's prided itself in having a large number of people over the age of 100. Specifically, the town had three times more centenarians than the rest of the country. The researchers looked into finding the similarities that these people had within the lives they lived. They tracked seven people aged from the 90s to early 100s, performing health check-ups and blood tests on them as well.

What they found out ended up being extremely interesting. All of them had higher levels of DHEA, a steroid hormone released by the adrenal glands that are said to be the longevity hormone. What's more, as they continued their research, they found out that they had several other things in common. Everyone had a hobby that they took part in each day that they loved doing: one woman spent hours each day carving traditional Japanese masks, one man enjoyed painting, and another liked to go fishing.

While they have yet to prove a connection between the higher levels of DHEA and a hobby, the program did suggest that having something that keeps you focused, interested and gives you a sense of satisfaction can boost DHEA. This could all mean that you live a longer and happier life.

Practitioners of Ikigai

Okinawa, an island off of mainland Japan, is home to one of the biggest ratios of centenarians to population. This also happens to be where the ikigai ideology calls home. They had mild weather, a healthy diet, and low-stress levels. It's the population of non-retiring, purpose-driven, active residents they have that connects them to communities in Sardinia, Italy, and the Greek island of Icaria, which are also known for their long-living communities.

Best-selling American author Dan Buettner took time to study different areas of the world where people lived a long time, including Okinawa, and found that, while each area had a different word to describe it, ikigai was an important link. However, the author and aspiring philosopher, Héctor García has said that ikigai doesn't have to just be linked to the elderly. In fact, a number of young people have found the importance of ikigai.

Having a Reason for Living

The ikigai Venn diagram also looks at the other intersection points besides the one in the center. There's an overlap between what you love and the things you are good at. This is where you would find what your passions are.

Then there's another overlap between the things you love and what the world needs. This could be seen as your mission. Where what the world needs and things that could make you money overlap would be seen as your vocation. Lastly, the area where the things you are good at and the things that can make you money overlap would be your profession.

To find the "sweet spot" of these things would be to figure out something that you're good at, you love to do, what the world needs, and people would pay you for it. For example, you could be passionate about helping out teens, you have skills that can help you with that, the world is in need of it, and your area has several jobs for it. You could easily say that you have discovered your ikigai.

Now, it's also important to understand that some people believe that this diagram is a Westernized creation of ikigai and not what ikigai was traditionally meant to be about. Traditionally, ikigai doesn't have to look at every section of that diagram. There are those who believe that your ikigai doesn't have to include things that help the world, or can earn you an income, or things that you do well. They believe that ikigai shouldn't be some "lofty and formidable goal to achieve." Instead, it's all about:

"Embracing the joy of little things, being in the here and now, reflecting on past happy memories, and having a frame of mind that one can build a happy and active life."

The traditional idea of ikigai doesn't have a lot to do with the "professional success of entrepreneurship." The traditional idea of ikigai is closely connected to Zen Buddhism and focuses on living in the moment, being active, finding flow, and finding joy in the little areas of your life.

The diagram we have discussed was created in 2014 by author and mentor Marc Winn. Three years after he came up with this idea, Marc said:

"In 2014, I wrote a blog post on the subject of ikigai. In that blog post, I merged two concepts to create something new. Essentially, I merged a Venn diagram on 'purpose' with Dan Buettner's ikigai concept in relation to living to be more than 100. The sum total of my effort was that I changed one word on a diagram and shared a 'new' meme with the world."

There was only one word changed? What is the Venn diagram about the purpose that he referenced? Winn further explained the source of the diagram originated with astrologer and author Andres Zuzunaga, who created a similar diagram in Spanish two years prior. Winn wanted to merge ikigai with Zuzunaga's concept of purpose. In the purpose diagram, you had the sections of:

- Four main circles:
- Lo que amas – what you love
- Lo que el mundo necesita – what the world needs
- Por lo que te pagaran – what they will pay you for
- Lo que haces bien – what you do well
- The overlaps were:
- Mission
- Profession
- Vocation
- Passion

However, could we say that Zuzunaga was the first person to create that? That would be difficult to do. These concepts are very close to the Hedgehog Concept created by the American business consultant and author Jim Collins in his book "Good to Great," published in 2001. He had a diagram with three circles that said:

- What drives your economic engine
- What you can be the best in the world at
- What are you deeply passionate about

The original Hedgehog Concept was made with business in mind, but it has since been updated to apply to people.

It doesn't matter if the ikigai diagram dates back to traditional ikigai teachings. Taking the time to fill out those sections is very useful and can give you some valuable insights into your values in life. Whether or not the middle of that diagram is your life's sweet spot remains to be seen, but it should help you figure out the things in life that make you happy.

Héctor García also said that studying ikigai ended up changing how he lives his life. He switched up the things that he did each morning so that he could begin his days doing what he felt was most important before tackling other things. Basically, he would prioritize his day based on what he felt was important. For some people, ikigai is career-focused, but it doesn't have to be about financial gain.

Living Ikigai

A famous Japanese chef, Jiro Ono, came up with an amazing illustration of ikigai. He explained that it was all about being devoted to the pursuit of something that makes you feel fulfilled and accomplished. Chef Ono chose to devote his time and efforts to perfecting sushi. He has a small, exclusive sushi restaurant in Tokyo that seats only ten people at a time.

He ended up earning a three-star Michelin rating and is known as one of the most accomplished sushi chefs in the world. A documentary was created about his life called *Jiro Dreams of Sushi*. In it, Chef Ono said, "You have to fall in love with your work, dedicate your life to mastering your skill. I'll keep trying to reach the top, but no one knows where the top is."

This is a fantastic example of what ikigai is all about and how you have to devote your time to do the things you love, work towards accomplishments and mastery, and the never-ending journey to fulfillment. The interesting thing about Chef Ono is that he not only manages the prep of the sushi, but he observes his customers as they eat his creations. He has changed how he makes his sushi based solely on how they react to it.

Jane Goodall, a famous primatologist, is another great example of living ikigai. At an early age, Goodall learned she was passionate about animals, especially primates. In her early 20s, she started writing to the anthropologist Louis Leakey, who thought that studying apes could help give us clues about early human ancestors.

Through Leakey, Goodall started to study apes. Much of what she learned was learned through working with the apes and documenting their intelligence and social interactions. This also meant that she became a big animal rights advocate, and she started to work to help save apes and other animals from having their habitats destroyed.

Goodall had the chance to pursue her passion, which meant she became very skilled at what she did and provided the world with a lot of important information about primates.

One last person who has done a great job at finding and living their ikigai is Dave Rostovich, a wildlife advocate and surfer. He became well-known for being a "free" surfer who had a lot of sponsorships, but he never took part in contests. He ended up founding the *Surfers for Cetaceans*, which works to protect cetaceans and other marine life animals.

Due to his love for surfing and the ocean, Rastovich began to admire the dolphins who would ride the waves along with him. He became used to a certain flow as he surfed. All of this taught him to appreciate the lives of these animals.

Discovering your ikigai or your reason for waking up happy is probably something a number of people are doing without knowing they are. While everybody's idea of what ikigai is will be different, there's a basic sense of agreement. That being, discovering a motivating purpose in life helps to bring you happiness and fulfillment.

We all have a basic need to pursue the things we are passionate about, make a living, help others, and develop our talents. It can be difficult to figure out where these things overlap, but with some self-reflection, it can be done.

Ikigai Misconceptions

We've already mentioned some of these in passing, but it's important to really look at these misconceptions so that they don't end up preventing you from discovering your ikigai. Also, the word misconception is used because while these things aren't required to find your ikigai, they may be a part of it. It all depends on you, so don't let these things discourage you.

- Ikigai does not have to be connected to work or money.

Human beings weren't born simply to work. Society is what has told us we must have a job and work. As such, it also means that ikigai doesn't have to be about your work or career. In 2010, a survey was given to 2000 Japanese people. They found that only about a third of the people saw their job as their ikigai. A person may see their job as their life's value, but it should not be limited to only that.

Also, you must look at the fact that a number of Japanese people continue to pursue their ikigai for their entire life. There are plenty of Japanese people who never retire. They continue to do what they love for as long as they can.

Other than work, a person's ikigai could be a spiritual feeling, a family, or a dream. It might also be a physical thing, like something you do, or it could simply be that you feel as though your life is worth living.

Since ikigai doesn't have to be your job, you can ignore the money aspect of the ikigai diagram if you would like to. As Westerners, we like to look at the money section as a quick way to figure out an ikigai because we're always looking for ways to make money. Money tends to lower the number of things that we do.

However, we shouldn't pigeonhole ourselves into only doing what can make us money. Figuring out your ikigai can be slow going if you get rid of this aspect, but it will end up being more meaningful.

- You don't have to look at ikigai for an all-or-nothing purpose.

A number of people out there are willing to try and convince you that you only have one life purpose. This is something that a lot of people struggle with because they think they must find that one thing that gives them purpose.

Author Iza Kavedizija said it best, "I have learned in my own research with older Japanese, what makes ikigai effective is its inextricable link to a sense of mastery – the idea known as 'chanto suru' that things should be done properly. As such, ikigai emphasizes process and immersion rather than a final aim."

- It's possible that you could have more than one ikigai.

It's important to remember that at any point in your life, you can choose to change your life purpose. It's normal and natural for a person's purpose to evolve.

The Ten Ikigai Rules

During their research of the centenarians of Okinawa, Héctor García and writer Francesc Miralles interviewed hundreds of people to help them understand their life philosophy and the secret to longevity. Through all of this, they created the ten rules of ikigai:

1. Follow your ikigai
2. Live in the moment
3. Stay active; don't retire

4. Give thanks
5. Take it slow
6. Reconnect with nature
7. Don't fill your stomach
8. Smile
9. Surround yourself with good friends
10. Get in shape for your next birthday

While we'll go over ways to find your ikigai, don't let yourself get discouraged if you start to struggle with the process. A great place to start is to write out a top ten list of everything you have done during the last week that you enjoyed. Then go through the list to mark the things that added purpose to your life. Don't let yourself get discouraged by feeling as if things are too permanent. Remember, your ikigai can change, just like your taste in food, music, and clothing has changed throughout your life.

two
your reason for getting up

VISUALIZE a time in your life when you will actually love waking up each morning because you are super excited about life. There isn't anything special about this particular day. You aren't going on your dream vacation. It isn't your birthday. It isn't your anniversary. It's just another ordinary day, and you are excited about it. You just can't wait to get your feet on the floor and get moving.

You might be wondering what in the world is happening. I am not talking about utopia or heaven but the feeling known as ikigai. This is what the Japanese refer to as their reason for being. This is basically an idea that I think every single person has.

Ikigai is basically the same as searching for your meaning in life. It's that one thing that brings you satisfaction, happiness, and purpose. Just like anything in life that's important to you, it isn't going to be simple. Figuring out your ikigai will be an enduring and deep search into your inner self. Plus, it just might be something that some might be already dealing with.

. . .

You'll be trying to find your passion, your purpose, and the things that make your life worth living while giving you the greatest joy each day.

One important difference is ikigai doesn't necessarily mean your economic status or your career, but it represents every aspect of your life like your spirituality, careers, relationships, hobbies, etc. It's the pinnacle of your entire life.

Ikigai can't be forced; it's something you want to do. They'll always be natural behaviors and actions. You aren't trying to be someone or something that you aren't.

How to Find Your Reason for Waking Up

This is not going to be an easy question to answer. It was created to stretch our minds. To cause an extremely deep look into how we live our lives. This is what makes up the foundation of the old principle of ikigai.

If you were to roughly translate ikigai, it would mean: "reason for which you wake up in the morning" or a bit simpler: "a reason for being."

Many people will live their whole life without taking the time to find this reason for being. Sarah Lewis, an art critic and historian said: "We are constantly wanting to close this gap between where we want to be and where we are." This gives us a very unique perspective when looking at our reasons for being. Everybody wants to know what they want to be as an adult, and everyone is trying their best to close this gap but is the place we WANT to be where we NEED to be?

Ikigai will be where your vocation, your profession, your mission, and your passion come together. This is a very delicate balance where you are supposed to live. Your reason for being will never be linked to economic status. In all reality, it is a set of spiritual and mental circumstances that you create for yourself.

The main reason why most people don't ever find theirs is that they have to put a lot of effort into it. We don't make an effort because we're too involved in growing our profession or career. We'll work our entire lives having an intention to find our passions and be able to do what we love after we have retired. This isn't the way it needs to be.

Dan Buettner from National Geographic once said: "Typically in America, we have divided our adult life up into two sections. There is our work life, where we are productive. And then one day, boom, we retire. And typically, that has meant retiring to the easy chair or going down to Arizona to play golf. In the Okinawan language, there is not even a word for retirement. Instead, there is one word that imbues your entire life, and that word is ikigai."

This isn't how anybody needs to go through their lives. You have to find the things you value in life. You have to find the things that make your life worth living. You need to find what fulfills your life. But you also need to take it a bit further. There isn't anything stopping you from finding your purpose in life for your business. It's just a system of living that can be translated into a larger sense outside of you.

There's been a lot said about how important it is for organizations to have an impact on their community. The impact is becoming more and more important, and there isn't any way you can deny this. Many companies are stressing the need for companies and organizations to impact their communities on a larger scale. The main reason we love impact is that it'll always line up with your vision. It should align with your company's passion. This is a part of your ikigai. Keep in mind that it's where your vocation, profession, mission, and passion all come together.

Helping people and organizations grow professionally and personally might be your "reason for being."

Your profession might be to help companies grow. Your vocation might be to teach other people how to grow. Your mission might be to help people grow no matter what. Your passion might be to create a global impact, so everybody has a chance to grow.

You need to find your delicate balance where you are meant to live. You need to find your ikigai. Have you ever thought about it? Have you ever thought about the "reason why you wake up each morning?" You have to find your personal reason for just being, and then you have to find your business's reason. Wonderful things are going to happen when you find this balance.

Reaching Ikigai

The questions listed below aren't really a part of the original concept of ikigai, but they could help you get on the right path:

- You Need to Find All the Things You Love

You need to try your best to ignore all the other things in the world when you answer this question. "What are some things you absolutely love to do?" You know what these are, but you might not know the things you need to do with them right at this moment. If you aren't completely sure, you can ask yourself this:

- What Are Some Things the World is in Need Of

If you can, take the time to think long and hard about this question. You might find some things the world is in need of. Just in your community, you can probably find some problems that you could help to solve. If you find a particular one that interests you, you could use this as your guide.

These next statements could help you find your ikigai. It could help create a foundation for these statements because they are more flexible.

- Find Things That Can Make You Money

If you are creative, you could make money doing just about anything. You just have to find the right people who are in need of what you are selling. Yes, you might have to get more creative, but there should be something of value in all the things that you love doing and what the world is in need of. You are just going to have to take some time to find it.

- Find All the Things That You Are Good At

Everybody is going to have some skills or traits that they are very good at. They might not want to do these things for the rest of their lives, or they might not like what they do, but if you look long and hard at yourself, you'll find some innate weaknesses and strengths.

If you don't really like what you're good at, you might just have to do these things a bit differently. If this still doesn't help, the best thing you can do is get better at it. With some time and effort, you could become great at many things. Putting in some effort and time is the key, and it might even be easy when you actually begin working on trying and getting better at all the things you love to do.

Putting all these things together will let you find various parts of yourself. Knowing the things you love and all the things you are good at will bring you to your passion. But figuring out what the world is in need of and the things you could get paid for will help you find your career.

Where all these things come together is where you'll reach your ikigai. This isn't something that'll happen in one day; it'll take most people years or their entire lives to find their passion, so figuring out your ikigai is going to be a lot harder.

. . .

Even if it is, it'll be the ultimate form of finding oneself. I hope these questions will help you begin discovering where you need to go to find your reason for being. So, will you be excited to get up tomorrow?

three
discovering your ikigai

THE JAPANESE HAVE the art of practicing kintsugi, which involves fixing broken pottery by filling the holes or cracks with gold leaf to make something that becomes more beautiful and valuable than the original. The object's imperfections become a part of its character and its beauty. The way we live both professionally and personally could get broken, too.

Ikigai can help us find our purpose. Much like kintsugi, it can create a more complete, fulfilling, and valuable new you.

Performing and enjoying an activity and your purpose in life is all ikigai and comes from a deep understanding of the following:

- Profession – what you could make money for
- Mission – what the world needs
- Vocation – what you are good at
- Passion – what you love

Journalist Yukari Mitsuhashi explains that ikigai isn't just about your overall life's meaning and goals, but it lives inside every single moment and your curiosity for every part of the way you live your life. The effects of ikigai could offer you a lot more than the way you live your life.

Because of this, there's been a lot of research about ikigai and the way to find your "reason for living," but also all of the health benefits that are associated with it. These positive benefits could be seen in various areas of your life that might include:

- Lowered incidences of cardiovascular disease
- Lowered chances of having a stroke
- Mental health
- Psychological well-being
- Physical health for the elderly

Since it does have a very complicated nature, it might be hard to figure out exactly what your ikigai is but lucky for you, there are various questionnaires online that could help you figure out what your ikigai is.

Ikigai-9 Questionnaire

This questionnaire can be used as a psychometric tool that is extremely convenient and reliable. It measures ikigai across many dimensions, including:

- Positive and active attitudes towards a person's future

- Acknowledgment of the meaning of a person's existence
- Positive and optimistic emotions towards life

This questionnaire has nine different statements that you will score against, so it makes it very simple to do. You just need to give yourself one point for every statement that you agree with.

1. I believe that I have some type of impact on a person.
2. I would live to further develop myself.
3. My life is mentally fulfilled and rich.
4. I think that my existence is needed by someone or something.
5. I am interested in many things.
6. I have room in my mind.
7. I feel that I am contributing to society or someone.
8. I would like to start something new or learn something new.
9. I often feel that I am happy.

Now that you have a way to measure ikigai, you will be able to understand, identify, and explore all the positive impacts of ikigai on your work and mental health.

Dispositional Flow Scale-2

Francesc Miralles and Hector Garcia write that while we can't have a guaranteed way to live our ikigai, flow is a major aspect that will allow us to "enjoy doing something so much that we forget about whatever worries we might have while we do it."

The sensation of optimal experience and flow is probably going to happen when the "demands of the task and the abilities of the performer are balanced."

The good news is that there is a widely accepted psychological tool called Dispositional Flow Scale-2. This can help measure a person's flow that has proven to be useful in several situations that range from playing video games to exercising. DFS-2 is used to measure the general tendency to get into the flow, rather than specific experiences, and looks at nine dimensions:

- Autotelic experience
- Time transformation
- Loss of self-consciousness
- Sense of control
- Concentration on the task
- Unambiguous feedback
- Clear goals
- Action-awareness merging
- Challenge-skill balance

Even though I can't give you a complete DFS-2 test, I am able to give you an excerpt from it. Every one of these statements will be connected to a certain activity, and you'll need to rate each one as: always, frequently, sometimes, rarely, or never.

When you are participating in (insert an activity),

1. I know exactly what I want to do.

2. I am completely focused on the things I am doing.
3. I am not worried about what other people think of me.
4. Things seem to be happening by themselves.
5. I find this experience to be extremely rewarding.

DFS-2 has been validated as an approach that is practical to measure flow and the ability to enter into an optimal psychological state. This puts them in the same flow as ikigai. Once you reach one of the psychological states of flow, it can help your daily tasks be a lot more exceptional.

Start Simply

The easiest way to begin finding your ikigai is by answering some simple questions. You'll find some questions below that you could answer to help you figure out your ikigai. You're going to need to separate your paper into four sections. One section will be titled "do what you love," the next section will be titled "do what you are good at," the third section will be titled "do something that you earn money for," and the last section will be titled "do something the world needs." You'll want to move from one question to the next in order. This will make it easier to figure out something where these things overlap because you will be taking things from the previous category and moving them into the next if they fit.

1. Do what you love – list out everything that you love to do and validate them with the following parameters:
2. What do you like doing in your spare time that makes you happy?

3. What did you like to do as a child or during your early adult years?
4. What do you never get bored doing?
5. What gets you into the flow?
6. Do what you are good at – looking at your answers in the previous section, move those in that list that you are good at into this list and validate them with these parameters:
7. What is it that people ask you to help them with?
8. Do you know what your skills and strengths are? What are they?
9. What skills have you been spending time practicing?
10. Is there something that you want to be good at?
11. Do something that you can earn money for – of those in the previous section, move the ones that you can get paid for into this category and validate them based on these parameters:
12. What job could you do?
13. What products or services could you sell?
14. What is something that you have been paid for before?
15. What would you like to get paid for?
16. What would you be doing if you didn't have your current job?
17. Do something the world needs – this is the trickiest thing for most people to figure out, and you will have to ponder this for a bit to figure what in the last category could be used to help change the world. To help you out, use the following to validate your answers:
18. What makes you frustrated or annoyed?
19. Who or what inspires you?
20. What do people around you need?
21. How could you contribute to a positive change?

Go through your answers and circle the common points that are present in each of your sections. This would be your ikigai. If you have multiple commonalities, then you may just have more than one ikigai. From here, you can begin looking at ways to use your ikigai to live a better life.

Passion

Where those things overlap, you will get four other areas. The first is Passion. If you find something that you're good at and that you love to do, then you know what your passion is. Some who are pursuing their passion are filled with a sense of happiness and satisfaction. However, others feel like what they are doing isn't creating a big enough impact or doesn't have any tangible rewards.

If that's your case, then you may need to figure out some ways where your passion can gain traction, grab the attention of others, or how it can make a difference in somebody's life. Moreover, if there's a way that you can make money with your passion, then that could help you connect in all four of the areas of ikigai.

For example, if you enjoy gardening and you're skilled at growing plants, then you may want to use those skills to create a small farm, which could earn you some money. You could also grow some ornamental flowers and plants and then sell them to other people.

Mission

When you have something you love, and the world needs it, then you have a mission. People who have a mission will usually become advocates for the things they believe in. They could become humanitarians who want to change the world by volunteering or offering free services to people in need. This can fill you with a sense of fulfillment. However, you may not be able to get proper compensation.

If this describes you, then you might not have figured out how to market your skills well. To be a professional in a certain field, you need more than a simple passion. You're also going to have to have proven knowledge and skill to help promote whatever it is that you support and love. This might be the reason why you haven't started earning any money while you dedicate yourself to your mission.

A good place to start is with some training. Formal education in the thing you love to do can make you even better at it. Given that it can already impact the world, you'll probably only need a little bit of time to make your craft a bit better, which will eventually boost your potential in becoming a full-blown expert.

After you have gained more knowledge, you can use your new skills and know-how to start earning money for the thing you love to do while also making a lasting impact on the world.

Profession

If you've something that you are good at and you make money for it, then you have found a profession. As a professional, you could be earning a lot of money doing something that you've mastered. These are the people who are typically considered experts, and this is the reason why they tend to be paid well.

But doing the things you are good at that makes you money doesn't always equal doing the things you love that affect the world. If you find yourself in a place in life where you've been working hard, but you don't have any sense of fulfillment, you may want to make some changes. To figure out your ikigai, you may need to figure out how your profession could become something you enjoy that helps other people.

For example, if you work in finance and you have a good reputation in a big company. You could use that network to create a charity, or you could start to raise money for the less fortunate. Your knowledge could also be helpful if you offered free coaching for small companies or trained other people who are interested in following in your footsteps.

Vocation

If you have something that you make money doing and something that might help the world, then you have a vocation. Some who have a vocation find that they aren't necessarily happy in what they're doing, and they might not be totally knowledgeable or an expert in their field.

. . .

If you feel like this describes you, then you need to figure out how you can get better at what you are doing and if you can turn it into something you love to do. You may want to start by getting a degree or signing up for classes that can help improve your skills. You can also try to get more experience in this field and eventually become an expert. After you've made this something you are really good at, you'll start to enjoy it a lot more.

Finding Your Purpose

Most people spend their entire day running on autopilot without ever thinking about what they're doing. They do everything they can to accomplish what they have to during the time that they're awake. They'll only stop to crash in front of the television, mindlessly watching whatever is on or going to bed. Ikigai tells us that we have to focus on our life's purpose and the "joy a person finds in living day-to-day."

Filling in the end of the following sentences could prove to be helpful in becoming clearer with regards to finding your life's purpose and how to focus your energy and time.

1. The following people inspire me because they...
2. If I were to be gone tomorrow, I would regret that I didn't...
3. If I were only given six months to live, I would spend my time...
4. In my free time, I love to...
5. If I didn't care what others thought of me, I would...
6. I am really good at...
7. I am most happy with who I am when I...

8. If I believed I could not fail, I would...
9. If money didn't matter, I would be...
10. When I was a child, I loved doing...

You can write multiple endings for these sentences, and you can add more as you think of them. Look over these sentences, and start to look for any patterns that start to emerge, and notice the actions that accompany your future plans and past activities. Once you do that, then you can finish this last sentence:

The purpose of my life is to...

That completed sentence should be used to consider and guide the future decisions that you make.

four
the importance of happiness

THE KEY ELEMENT of ikigai is helping you find happiness. But happiness is a pretty big word with lots of meaning. In this context it's all about the emotional state that includes feelings of contentment, satisfaction, fulfillment, and joy. While we all have our own definitions of happiness, most of the time, it's seen as experiencing positive emotions and being satisfied with what you have.

When it comes to talking about happiness, a person could be talking about how they currently feel, or they could be speaking in general about how they feel in life. Since happiness is usually defined broadly, social scientists and psychologists tend to talk about it as "subjective well-being." Much like how "subjective well-being" sounds, it focuses on the overall feel of the person that they are experiencing in the present.

There are two main aspects of this:

1. Balanced Emotions – We are all going to feel negative and positive emotions at some point. Happiness has been connected with getting to experience more positive things than negative.
2. Satisfaction with Life – This involves how satisfied you are with the different aspects of your life, which could include achievements, work, relationships, and everything else that you view as important.

What are some good ways to know whether or not you are feeling happy? While we all have a different happiness perception, there are some basic signs that psychologists look for in people when assessing how happy they may be. Common happiness signs include:

- Being satisfied with life
- Feeling like they have accomplished, or will accomplish, things they want
- They experience more positives than negatives
- They feel they are living the life they want
- Feeling as though their living conditions are good

You have to remember that happiness doesn't mean that you are constantly in a state of euphoria. Instead, happiness is about having an overall sense of feeling more positive than negative. Even when a person is mainly happy, they may still experience an entire range of emotions that include boredom, loneliness, sadness, frustration, and anger. Even when faced with discomfort, they will have a better underlying sense of optimism that things will get better. They know that they can handle whatever is going on.

Different Types of Happiness

The feeling of happiness may not vary much, but the way in which we think about happiness can vary, and that's how we have different types of happiness. For example, Greek philosopher Aristotle distinguished between Hedonia and Eudaimonia.

Hedonia is that type of happiness that comes from pleasure. You feel this when you do things that feel good to you, like acts of self-care, as well as feeling satisfied, experiencing joy, and fulfilling your desires.

Eudaimonia is the type of happiness where you find meaning and virtue in life. The biggest aspect of eudiamonic well-being includes feelings of value, purpose, and meaning. It's very close in relation to living up to your ideals, concern for others, achieving long-term goals, and fulfilling responsibilities.

In today's world, psychologists call eudaimonia and hedonia meaning and pleasure, respectively. They have also found a third type of happiness that is connected with engagement. This type of happiness is found by taking part in different aspects of your life.

Research has discovered that happy people often experience more eudaimonic satisfaction and will normally have a better than average rank of hedonic satisfaction. This is a very important player in the way in which a person experiences happiness, but the value of these things is subjective. What one person sees as pleasurable, another might not.

·   ·   ·

The following are different types of happiness that could be categorized into the three main forms of happiness:

- Pride – this is experienced by feelings of satisfaction in things that you have finished
- Contentment – this is experienced by feelings of satisfaction
- Optimism – this is experienced by how you look at life, usually with an upbeat outlook
- Gratitude – this is experienced through positive emotions that involve feelings of thankfulness
- Joy – this is experienced as a fleeting moment of happiness that is felt in the moment
- Excitement – this is experienced by happy feelings that involve feeling happy about something that is going to happen

Now, let's take those things and look at them a little bit more closely.

Joy

Joy can be experienced when you lose yourself in the moment and appreciate the things you have. This is very fleeting and tends to sneak up on you. It also disappears if you start overanalyzing it. The good news is that you can find joy in a number of different things if you keep the right perspective and attitude, so it's one of the easiest types of happiness that you can look for.

. . .

The easiest way to bring joy into your life is to do something that makes you feel joy. This might be going to a theme park or going to a yoga class. A great way to discover joy is to start doing different things.

Excitement

Excitement often lasts longer than joy does, but it can still be fleeting. Whatever it is that you are anticipating, once it's passed, the excitement will also disappear. However, it can also serve as a motivator. Being excited about a job can give you the motivation you need to work harder. If your relationship brings you excitement, you will be more motivated to work through problems you may have.

Excitement helps to calm down jitters. Studies have found that when you tell yourself you are excited instead of anxious, you can make a channel for uncomfortable energy to make it constructive. Excitement can extend the positive emotions you have towards certain things. For example, getting excited about a vacation can help to extend that happy feeling for days or weeks beforehand. It's also one of the easiest forms of happiness to find. A bucket list is a great way to feel the excitement.

Gratitude

This type of happiness will disappear if you don't work at it. This is one of the most important types of happiness that a person should seek out. Those who feel gratitude on a regular basis tend to be healthier and happier than people who don't.

Plus, it's also very easy to cultivate gratitude. You can let a person know that you appreciate them. A lot of people will keep a gratitude journal and write in it each day. Finding gratitude in your life helps stave off the effects of depression and other forms of mental illness. It's also one of the less obvious forms of happiness.

Pride

Pride is a tricky form of happiness because it can become negative, such as with competitive or smug pride. However, feelings of pride in things you've accomplished can help you turn gratitude inward. You can find pride in your work and family, home, yourself, and anything else that you can put effort into.

Cultivating healthy amounts of pride can be accomplished by writing out the accomplishments you've made or listing out "wins." This is not the same thing as bragging or "being full of yourself." Taking pride in yourself doesn't mean that you think you're better than others. Rather, you have reached a better version of yourself.

Optimism

There are studies that have connected optimism with a better life. Optimists focus on possibilities, and they experience a combination of pride and gratitude. They feel grateful about the chances they get, believe in themselves, and are proud of all of their abilities.

Optimists who face disappointment can minimize it and look for ways to do better. They'll spot possible issues that might have contributed to the unfortunate outcome. When they do good, they are willing to take credit for their success, and they know that great things are coming their way. Optimism is often a way of life for people, so it tends to be a lasting form of happiness.

Contentment

Contentment is all about feeling happy with what you have. People who experience this often experience less disappointment with life's drawbacks, and they tend to feel lucky to have the things they do.

People will often work towards finding this type of happiness. It often occurs when a person chooses to focus on gratitude for what they have, and they feel as though they deserve the rewards they get. Reveling in what you accomplished is a great way to feel contentment, so try to focus on things you have to find contentment.

Love

This wasn't on the above list, but happiness and love tend to be used interchangeably. There are people who believe that love can give us an infinite source of happiness. Happiness also serves as a form of love. However you look at it, it's an important form of happiness to have. Television often makes love look like it's hard to find, but love can easily be found. You don't have to have romantic relationships to find love. It can be found within the family, friendships, and even relationships with pets. When you focus on these relationships, it can bring a lot into your life. This is a type of happiness that can give you an endless amount of happiness.

How to Find Happiness

While there are those people who seem to be naturally happy, there are ways you can cultivate more happiness. Large-scale studies performed on twins have found that about 10 percent of life satisfaction came from external events, 50 percent came from genetics, and the other 40 percent came from things the person engaged in.

While you can't control what your "base level" of happiness is, there are some things that you can do that can up your feelings of happiness and live a more fulfilling life. The happiest person alive will experience moments of feeling down, but happiness is something that we can constantly pursue.

A great way to do that is to learn what your ikigai is. The following tips tie into your ikigai and can help you feel more excited for the day.

- Go after your goals

Achieving things that are internally motivated, especially those that help you grow can give you a big happiness boost. Some research has found that pursuing goals that are internally moti-vated can help to improve your happiness more so than goals that are externally motivated, like gaining money or status.

- Enjoy every moment

There are studies that have found that humans tend to over-earn. We focus a lot on accumulating things, which causes us to lose sight of enjoying what we have. Instead of falling into this trap, try to practice gratitude for what you already have.

- Find a sense of purpose

This is a big player in the ikigai world. Research suggests that people who feel as though their life has purpose will have better well-being and feel more fulfilled. When you have a sense of purpose, you feel as though your life has meaning, direction, and goals. It helps a person's happiness because it helps them make better decisions.

A few things that you can do to figure out what your sense of purpose includes:

- Looking for something new that you would like to learn more about
- Fight against injustices
- Take part in altruistic and prosocial causes
- Explore your passions and interests

Your sense of purpose can be greatly influenced by many things, but you can improve this aspect of yourself. It means that you take the time to find a goal that you care a lot about that is going to cause you to engage in positive and productive actions to reach the goal.

- Share gratitude

One study had its participants perform a writing exercise every evening before they went to bed. Some of them were told to write about troubles they experienced during the day. Another group was asked to write about neutral events. The others were asked to write about things they were grateful for. Those who had written about things they were grateful for had higher levels of positive emotions, increased happiness, and more life satisfaction.

It was concluded that if a person kept a gratitude list, it could help to boost a person's overall mood. Try setting aside some time every evening to write out the things you are grateful for.

- Reframe the negatives

If you tend to be stuck in a more pessimistic view of things or you're feeling negative, try to find ways to reframe those thoughts. It is normal for people to have a negative bias where you focus on more negative things. This impacts the decisions you make and how you form impressions of others. When you discount the positives, it can contribute to an overall negative mindset.

. . .

When you take the time to reframe these negative perceptions, it doesn't mean that you simply ignore the bad things. Instead, you are taking on a more balanced and realistic view of things. It allows you to spot patterns in your thinking and challenge your negative thoughts as they come up.

Finding a Sense of Purpose

Since finding purpose in life is a great way to find happiness, let's look at how you can find your purpose. Remember that a lot of what we've already discussed in this book can help guide you towards your purpose in life.

The first thing to try is to donate your time, talent, or money. Helping others in some way is a great place to start in finding your purpose. Altruistic actions include donating items, volunteering, or just helping a person during their day.

Whether you'd like to spend a few Saturdays giving out meals, or if you drive the elderly to the grocery store once a week, doing things to help others can help you find meaning in life.

Another way to find your purpose is to listen to what others say. It's sometimes difficult to spot the things that you're passionate about. There are probably a lot of things you like to do, and you might have become so used to those things that you probably don't realize you find them important. Fortunately, others can give you a bit of insight. You have probably already started to show signs of passion or purpose to those around you, and you likely don't even know it.

· · ·

Ask a friend or a person you trust, and see what reminds them of you. It also wouldn't hurt to pay attention to what you are doing when a person pays you a compliment. Jot down these things and try to spot some patterns.

The third thing you can do to find purpose is to ensure you are surrounded by positive people. What are some common interests you have with the people you are around? Don't think about the people you feel obligated to be around, like family or co-workers. Look at those you chose to be with or like spending time with outside of mandatory functions. Those are the ones you have chosen to have in your life, and they say a lot about you. If most of the people you're around tend to be more positive, then you'll likely be more positive. The opposite is also true, and those people will often drag you down with them. In that case, you may have some changes that need to be made.

Lastly, start exploring your interests. Is there something that you like to talk about a lot? What things do you share about the most online? Think about conversations you have with others. The things that you like to share and talk about can often reveal some things that can give you purpose.

Happiness Challenges

While finding happiness is an admirable goal, there are going to be times when you may fall short. Let's go over some challenges you may face when it comes to finding happiness.

- Placing value on the wrong things

I can't tell you what to value in life, but there are some things that are only going to create more problems in the long run. We've all been told that money can't buy happiness. However, there are studies that have found that spending money on experiences can give you happiness, more so than buying physical things.

There was another study that found spending money on things that help to save your time can improve your happiness levels and satisfaction in life. Instead of placing more value on physical possessions, money, or statues, pursue goals that'll give you more free time or enjoyable experiences.

- Not seeking out social support

To have social support means that you have people in your life who you trust to be there when you need them the most. There are studies that have discovered that social support plays a huge role in the well-being of a person. For example, one study discovered that the perception of social support made up half of a person's overall happiness.

An important aspect of social support is that the quality of the support is a lot more important than how many people you have in your life. Having just a couple of close and trusted friends will do more good than barely knowing a bunch of people.

- Believing that happiness has an endpoint that can be reached

Happiness isn't just a goal that you are trying to reach and then be done. It's something that has to be constantly pursued that requires nurturing and sustenance. One study discovered that people who placed more value on happiness were often those who felt the least satisfied with their life. Basically, they put happiness on such a high pedestal that they think it's impossible to reach.

When you place too much value on happiness, it can become a self-defeating goal. This is due to the fact that the greater the odds are that you will feel disappointed when it doesn't meet the expectations you had for it. Perhaps, it may be more important to not make something as broad as happiness your goal. Instead, focus on building the relationships in life that will help you feel satisfied and fulfilled.

five
using meditation

MEDITATION HAS STARTED to gain more traction and attention over the past several decades, including statements by successful people who swear by its efficacy. In Japan, they practice what's known as Zazen. It is a form of seated meditation. But the benefits of meditation have spread much farther than in Japan. The Mayo Clinic, a non-profit global leader in medical care, research and education, has even written articles on how meditation can help improve your happiness, slow down time, and reduce stress.

Meditation is a form of mindfulness. Mindfulness has its roots in Buddhism, dating back thousands of years to Buddha himself. (See *Buddhism for Beginners* by Ramis Kachar for a good overview on Buddhism). The practice of mindfulness means that you focus your attention on the present moment. When you practice mindfulness, it helps you develop a good sense of wisdom, being, and self-knowledge. This allows you to get rid of, or see beyond, superficial preoccupations. It helps to direct your attention to the smaller things in life and sometimes to the more important things. Much like a compass, it can help you navigate through the journey of life and aims you towards meaningfulness and enlightenment. Therefore, it shouldn't be a surprise that a lot of mindful meditations can help you cultivate a purpose in your life which is your ikigai.

As we have covered, the concept of ikigai is following your purpose in life. It's where giving, social well-being, skills, and passions converge. Where all of these things intersect is where you can find your purpose.

However, to move past passion and work towards a deeper sense of purpose, it's important that you're in the right state of mind. Mindful meditation can help you get there.

This form of meditation is a fairly easy form of mindfulness, and you can pretty much do it anywhere you want. There are two forms of mindful meditations that you can choose to do.

1. You can do internal mindfulness, where you spend some time clearing your mind of clutter. You deliberately dedicate your thoughts inwards towards the way you feel in a certain moment.
2. You can do external mindfulness, where you spend a bit of time taking in everything around you. Your thoughts are more focused on what you are doing and how the things you do could affect the people around you. This form of meditation helps you appreciate each moment and allows you to fully experience your life.

Both of those forms of mediations can take a bit of time to get used to, but when you make a habit of it, you can get more comfortable with the practice. With time, you'll start to see the benefits of this mindful meditation and how it can help you find your ikigai.

Mindfulness of Your Health

Ikigai isn't all about your desires or passions to change the world. It's about living. Ikigai encompasses you completely. Your purpose in life is all about keeping strong in your well-being and mental health, which is the reason mindful meditation can help you.

When you are mindful of your surroundings, it can help you to relieve a lot of anxiety and stress that external things create that you don't have much control over. Essentially, when you are mindful of the things that are out of your control, you can gain a more objective view of what is going on.

When you have an objective view of things, it helps you to identify the barriers that stand between where you are and where you would like to be. When you can recognize your surroundings, it will reveal the things that influence them the most. New opportunities and ways of working through the hard times will become clearer, as well as the method in which you handle them.

When you have this type of mindful view on the things that are outside of you, you'll find that you can more easily manage your emotions, both negative and positive. When you do this, internal mindfulness can help relax your muscles and reduce hypertension, which will help improve your physical health.

. . .

Furthermore, when you understand your own thoughts, it can lead to acknowledging how you feel. What's more important is that internal mindfulness can help you consider the reasons you might feel a certain way and how you plan on proceeding, changing directions, or stopping altogether. It allows you to better serve your purpose in life if you're in the right mind space.

Be Mindful of the Things You Eat

Just like how mindfulness can improve your mental well-being, it's just as important to be mindful of the things that you allow into your body. Basically, you need to take care of your physical self, particularly when it comes to the things you eat and how much you consume.

The Bill and Melinda Gates Foundation did a study called, "health effects of dietary risks in 195 countries, 1990 – 2017: a systemic analysis for the Global Burden of Disease Study 2017." In this study, they found that there is a direct correlation between life expectancy rates and healthy diets.

The study also made it clear that diets with a low sodium intake and a high intake of fruits and whole grains could help prevent health problems. When a person consumes a suboptimal diet, it can be more detrimental to their health than other things like smoking. Also, it helps when a person is mindful of the number of calories they consume. They don't feel the need to stuff themselves. They eat to live, and they don't live to eat. It should come as no surprise, but overeating is the main cause of obesity.

. . .

Furthermore, when you are mindful of how often you exercise, it can help improve your health. You must exercise on a regular basis and keep yourself fit. One of the most important aspects of your life should be your health. Without your health, it's pretty hard to get anything else done, let alone work towards your dreams and passions.

Mindfulness Helps You See Things as They Are

Living in the moment is relaxing. It creates a door to your surroundings without distractions or preconceptions. Mindfulness gives you the chance to eliminate or see beyond the superficial aspects of life. It keeps your attention directed to the smaller and more important things in life.

With every positive feeling, sensation, and absence of distraction, you place yourself in a more relaxed state that facilitates a higher level of concentration in the things you do. This type of self-reflection can help you to figure out your ikigai.

When you practice mindfulness, it helps to shed light on your rationality and thoughts. This reflection provides you with a path towards acceptance based on meaning. It helps to improve your well-being and provides you with a more satisfying life. There will be a lower chance that you'll feel anxious about the future or regret the things you did in the past.

Plus, it helps you accept the present moment, whether it be negative or positive, and it helps to reduce any tendency to pass judgment or any biases. When you are mindful about seeing things as they are, it will help you to align your beliefs and values.

That doesn't mean you have to accept or agree with your situation.

You should never give up your principles for the sake of inaction or neutrality. If you feel as though growth or change is needed within a society or for you on a personal level, then you should act on that feeling. Being mindful is going to provide you with a clearer purpose.

The Beginner Mindset

Those who have been learning about their ikigai and working towards it for a while will tell you that the secret to happiness is to remain like a child and to have a "beginner's mind." Basically, you should keep an attitude of openness and eagerness to learn new things even if you've been working on them for years. When you have that curiosity, it'll ensure that you can continue to push forward and will never allow yourself to become stuck.

Practicing mindfulness at the start of your journey is probably one of the most important aspects of learning about your ikigai. When you are starting out, you won't have ingrained opinions, which means you will likely be more receptive to new possibilities and ideas. Lacking any prior experience means that you aren't going to have a bunch of habits to break or biases to unlearn, and you will be willing to listen to others.

Of course, keeping the child mindset can be difficult for people who have years of experience. It can be hard to push aside the things that you know and empty the mind to accept something new. When you have ingrained habits, it's hard to start doing things in a different way.

· · ·

However, this should serve as a way to strengthen your need to make more of an effort to be mindful. At this point, you will begin to be more mindful and set aside your excuses.

Practice Patience

Practicing mindfulness gives you the ability to appreciate your purpose in life without the need to be rewarded and recognized. Your life is going to be filled with targets, indicators, and benchmarks to measure your level of success, whether you like it or not. It's natural to want to feel some sense of accomplishment or gratification. Just think about all of those times where you have pushed yourself into doing things. After you reached your desired outcome, you had the chance to bask in the glory of your accomplishments.

If you were unable to reach your desired outcome, you probably felt some negative feelings which caused your motivation to drop. This is a false sense of ikigai.

Yes, there is satisfaction from winning at something. However, ikigai doesn't demand you to always find satisfaction in winning. There won't ever be a time where you accomplish something and feel bad. You forever follow your passions because you love the things you do. Don't ever stop. You keep pushing forward because ikigai is for life. It'll be there forever and always, motivating you when you need it.

Meditation can help release you from looking towards superficial things and instill you with a greater sense of patience. As you become more patient and you no longer need instant gratification, you will allow yourself to focus on what brings more meaning into your life.

. . .

You will become more comfortable with how much time it takes to develop skills. Meditation and mindfulness help you to dive deeper inside yourself and find that sense of satisfaction in the things that you do. With time, your understanding and passion for why you do these things will become clearer.

Be Mindful

Mindfulness is another form of meditation that can have a number of positive impacts on your life. The best way to be more mindful is to start paying attention to the things that are going on around you and inside of you. You have to make a conscious effort of practicing and forming a habit of being in the moment. Yes, it'll be a bit difficult when you first start out, but it'll get easier with time.

When you start being more mindful, you'll start seeing patterns in your actions, what you are more mindful of, and the things that you aren't. It'll allow you to create new skills and improve your overall well-being. Removing preconceived notions that you may have and other conditions that you have hung onto will be easier to get rid of.

It's important that you pay attention to the moments where you find yourself really enjoying what's going on. Reflect on how these moments made you feel. Notice them, and try to repeat those moments as often as you can. You might start to realize that you are moving towards a happier life with more purpose, which is ultimately the goal of ikigai.

six

accepting who you are

YOU HAVE MADE the decision to live an ikigai life. You need to know that self-awareness and self-acceptance are two areas that you are going to have to explore. You're going to need to get to know yourself better. You need to understand how your past experiences and childhood have influenced every single thing that you believe.

Once you are able to accept yourself for who you truly are, you have to realize that it doesn't matter what happened in your past because you can't go back and change anything. You are only able to control who you are at this very moment. You can't allow the traumas from your past to influence how you see and feel about yourself now. You need to have courage and learn to love yourself as you are if you really want to live the ikigai life.

Are you ready to accept yourself?

This might sound like a weird question because you might be wondering what accepting yourself really looks like? You are probably thinking that self-acceptance is something that everyone does naturally.

I'm here to tell you that being able to accept yourself isn't something that automatically happens. Many people are going to have problems accepting themselves as they are. It won't ever be hard to accept the good qualities about yourself, but what about all those annoying habits that others find fault with? But don't we have to accept all our flaws and failures?

Yes, we do. This is what you need to do. Read on to find out why you need to accept yourself, including all the bad and good. You'll find some practical tips that can help you accomplish this.

Self-Acceptance and What it Means

If you look at the word, you can pretty much determine what its definition is going to be: "the state of complete acceptance of oneself." If you want to completely accept who you truly are, you are going to need to embrace everything about you without any conditions, exceptions, or qualifications.

If you want a more academic definition: "Self-acceptance is a person's acceptance of all their attributes, whether they be positive or negative."

This helps you know the importance of accepting every facet of your being. You can't just embrace and accept all the positive, good, and valuable things about yourself. If you want to truly have self-acceptance, you have to accept all the negative, ugly, and less desirable parts of your being.

. . .

If you think that accepting all those negative things about you is going to be hard to do, you are totally right. It's not going to be an easy task accepting all those things that you want to forget about or change. You can only begin improving yourself after you have completely accepted who you really are.

This basically is saying that you have to understand and acknowledge that you have traits and habits that you don't like before you ever think about starting a journey to improve yourself.

Accepting Yourself Unconditionally

In order to have a good beginning on changing yourself, you have to begin by accepting yourself. You have to truly accept yourself unconditionally. It is easy to accept yourself when you do something great, like when you get your dream job, you get a promotion, you find your soul mate, or you win an award. But you also have to accept yourself when you are at your lowest, when all your faults and flaws are out in the open. This is when you have to truly accept yourself.

Clinical psychologist Russell Grieger says that accepting yourself unconditionally is understanding that you are a completely separate being from all your actions and qualities. You have to accept the fact that you have flaws and you have made and are going to make mistakes. But you also have to realize that these things don't define who you really are.

. . .

Russell says: "You accept that, as a fallible human being, you are less than perfect. You will often perform well, but you will also err at times... You always and unconditionally accept yourself without judgment."

When you begin practicing self-acceptance, you can begin loving yourself, embracing who you really are, and working on improving all those undesirable traits and qualities.

Self-Esteem Versus Self-Acceptance

Although self-acceptance has been closely related to all the other "self" concepts, it does have some elements that are unique to it. Self-esteem is an extremely close relative, and it works with all the other relationships you have with yourself, but they differ in very important ways. When you are talking about self-esteem, we are talking about how you feel about yourself. This might mean you think you are valuable, good, and worthwhile, but accepting yourself is just accepting and acknowledging that you are only going to be who you truly are.

Although self-esteem usually refers to how valuable we see ourselves, self-acceptance takes it one step farther to a global affirmation about yourself. Once we are able to accept ourselves, we'll be able to embrace every facet of ourselves and not just the positive parts.

Using Self-Acceptance in Therapy

When you don't have any self-acceptance, it's usually caused by low levels of well-being, and can lead to mental health problems, or alternatively, be created by mental illnesses. Because low self-acceptance could cause or be created by mental illnesses, it does make sense that accepting yourself more could create a protective barrier against all your negative experiences. Just knowing that you can build yourself a quality foundation for better mental health due to all the science behind self-acceptance could help build your self-confidence enough to give you a mental boost.

For anyone who has seen a therapist, you may have talked about the importance of accepting yourself and your reality. Those exact words might not have been used, and it's likely that your therapist helped you work on acknowledging both the bad and good inside you. They helped you accept every aspect of who you are and helped you learn how to separate all the things you do from who you truly are.

Let me take a minute to point out something very important that you have to know when you are trying to accept yourself for who you are: if you want to really accept yourself and all of your mistakes and flaws it doesn't mean you actually approve of these actions, traits, and characteristics but you are just accepting the fact that you know about these things and they are just another part of your true self.

You've to be able to make this distinction because some people who are in therapy struggle with this idea of accepting every horrible thing about themselves, what they do, or how they feel. This makes them feel like they have done horrible things, although they haven't. Being able to accept your reality for what it really is doesn't mean you have to approve of your reality. You'll always have room for growth.

.   .   .

You also have to accept the fact that all the things you have done in your past doesn't mean you are celebrating or that you like everything about yourself. You just have to accept that these less desirable parts of yourself are a part of you, and there isn't anything you can do about them. They don't define you anymore, and they don't make you less of a person. They are your past, and you are moving forward to better yourself.

An experienced therapist can help you learn how to accept yourself while giving you the support you need to help you build your self-acceptance while focusing on making yourself better. Your therapist can even give you some tools to help you accept yourself easier during therapy.

Some therapists might suggest you go to special group therapy. During these workshops, the therapist will put everyone into a type of hypnotic trance. While the people are in a trance, it's easier for them to accept every aspect of themselves while enhancing their self-awareness. This type of therapy is very new, and there isn't a lot of evidence that shows if it's a useful type of therapy. If this sounds like something you would be willing to try, talk to your therapist or general practitioner about trying it.

Self-Acceptance Examples

By now, you know what self-acceptance is and the way it can benefit you. Let's move on: "What does self-acceptance look like?" and "How do we know when we have reached self-acceptance?"

. . .

When you look at yourself in the mirror every morning, do you accept the wonderful, unique work in progress that is looking back at you?

You're going to know when you reach self-acceptance because you'll be able to see yourself in that mirror every morning and love everything you see. You'll accept every tiny bit of everything that makes you and who you were born to be. When you don't try to explain, ignore, or mitigate any flaws or faults, whether they are mental or physical, you have reached self-acceptance.

Self-acceptance is going to look different for everyone. It all depends on the thing you've struggled with and the pieces of yourself that you don't want to think about anymore. Let's take a look at a couple of examples of self-acceptance:

- A man might be going through a divorce, and he feels like he has failed. For this situation, his form of self-acceptance could look like acknowledging that there were some mistakes that he made in the marriage, but that doesn't mean that he, as a person, is a failure.
- A woman who has struggled with an eating disorder might accept that she has a human body that isn't perfect. She might acknowledge that she approached her imperfections by trying to deal with them in a harmful manner. She is committed to working on this harmful manner.
- A teenager is struggling with low self-esteem. She could ignore facing the self-defeating thought and beliefs she has and could reach self-acceptance if she can confront and acknowledge her cognitive distortions and negative beliefs.

- A new employee is struggling to meet all the goals that their demanding boss has set for them and might accept themselves by accepting the fact that sometimes they are not going to be able to reach certain goals. However, they are still a good person even though they might fail at times.

afterword

Thank you for making it through to the end of *The Ikigai Book* - let's hope it was informative and able to provide you with all of the tools you need to achieve your goals whatever they may be.

The next step is to start using the information we've gone over to help you discover your ikigai. A lot of things change in our lives, and it can be difficult to find normalcy. With ikigai and self-acceptance, you can ride those waves with more confidence. You'll no longer feel at the mercy of what life throws at you. You'll know your purpose and what gets you up each morning, and you'll be ready to face the day.

Finally, if you found this book useful in any way, a review is always appreciated!

Further Reading
   Go check out my other books where I'm exploring life happiness in other countries:

The Hygge Book: Living a Happy Life the Danish Way.

The Lagom Book: A Balanced and Happy Life from Sweden.

And as previously mentioned:

Buddhism For Beginners - Beginner's Guide To Understanding And Practicing Buddhism And How Buddhist Meditation Can Help You Achieve Enlightenment. - by Ramis Kachar

Printed in Great Britain
by Amazon